# Tales Of The Forbidden Island Of
# NI'IHAU

## LAWRENCE KAINOAHOU GAY

FIRST PRINTING

Library of Congress Cataloging in Publication Data Number
applied for:

Gay, Lawrence

  Tales of The Forbidden Island Of Ni'ihau
  1. Gay, Lawrence

ISBN 0-914916-43-2 paperback

Manufactured in the United States of America

Published by
TOPGALLANT PUBLISHING CO., LTD.
845 Mission Lane
Honolulu, Hawaii 96813

*This book is for my wife, Mary Helen Lindsey Gay*

*Tales Of The Forbidden Island Of*

TOPGALLANT PUBLISHING CO., LTD. - HONOLULU, HAWAII

# NI'IHAU

## LAWRENCE KAINOAHOU GAY

**Island of Ni'ihau** *as viewed from Kauai*
*Bernice P. Bishop Museum Photo*

# CONTENTS

Fault line scarp forming the eastern face of Niʻihau lava dome remnant.
W. D. Hohenthal, Bernice P. Bishop Museum Photo

# PREFACE

I was always interested with the island of Ni'ihau which was bought by my great-grandmother in 1864 from King Kamehameha V.

My father, Charles Gay told my sister Amelia and I many interesting stories about the Sinclair and Gay families. Grandmother Jane Sinclair Gay also told my father many stories about their family and their experiences in New Zealand, Honolulu and Ni'ihau.

I have been asked by many people of the State of Hawai'i about the island of Ni'ihau and why outsiders are not allowed to go there, so I told them I had planned to write a book about that island with stories told to me by my father and some friends who knew our family.

James Gay, one of Captain Gay's great-grandsons by his former marriage did some research work on Captain Gay's life. He gave me some valuable information from the Mitchell Library of New Castle, New Zealand regarding Captain Thomas Gay.

Reverend Alfred Chu Hing of Hawaiian-Chinese ancestry told me he used to go to Ni'ihau once in three months to conduct the church services to the Ni'ihauans. He said the people there were very friendly and whenever he returned to Maui, they would present him with fish and other delicacies.

I wish to express my sincere appreciation to those who gave me valuable information about the island of Ni'ihau, especially to my sister Amelia and also to Susan Thaner of the photo department of the Archives, for the interesting photographs of the island of Ni'ihau.

Grateful acknowledgement to my wife, Mary Helen Lindsey Gay for her help, patience and interest in making this book a reality.

Lawrence Kainoahou Gay

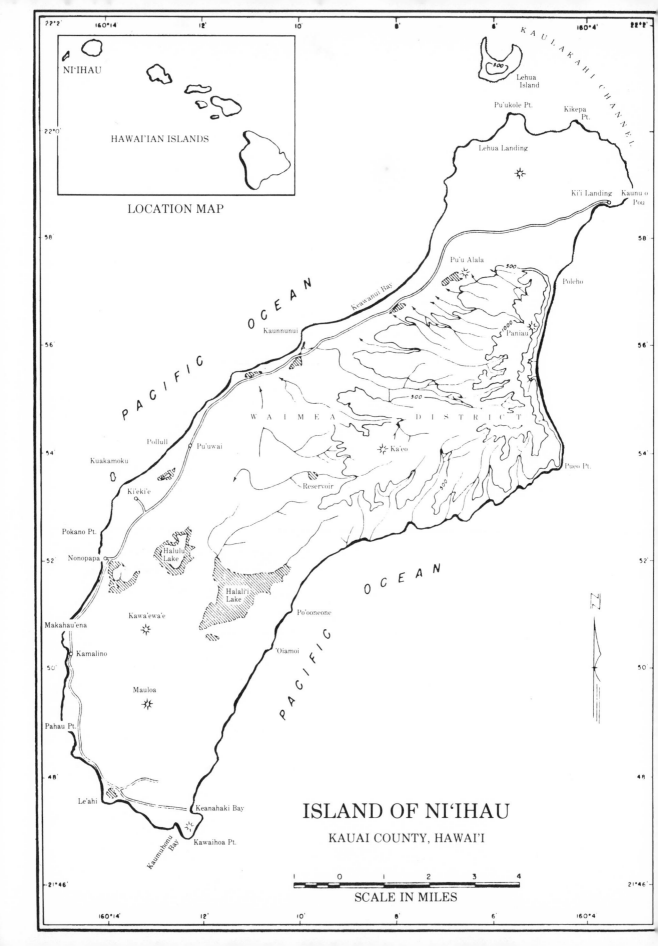

LOCATION MAP

HAWAI'IAN ISLANDS

NI'IHAU

# ISLAND OF NI'IHAU

## KAUAI COUNTY, HAWAI'I

SCALE IN MILES

# Tales Of The Forbidden Island Of
# NI‘IHAU

## LAWRENCE KAINOAHOU GAY

2

LAWRENCE KAINOAHOU GAY

# LAWRENCE KAINOAHOU GAY

## Author of the
## Tales Of The Forbidden Island Of Niʻihau

LAWRENCE KAINOAHOU GAY was born at Waimea, Kauaʻi, eldest son of Charles and Louisa Gay. He was educated at Punahou School and the University of California at Davis and was connected with the Mills' Orchard Corporation at Hamilton City, California, before entering the service in the First Marine Aviation, U.S. Marine Corps at Miami, Florida during World War I.

On February 28, 1919 he was transferred to inactive duty and returned to Lanaʻi to fulfill his father's request to help him with the operation of his ranch. Shortly before the sale of Gay's Ranch to the Hawaiian Pineapple Company (now Dole's) he became associated with the Extension Division of the University of Hawaiʻi. Two years later he became associated with the Board of Agriculture and Forestry, in the division of Entomology. For the past twenty five years he has done extensive research work into the annals of Hawaiʻi. He was the author of "True Stories of the Island of Lanaʻi".

# CHARLES GAY

CHARLES GAY, father of Lawrence Gay, was born January 8, 1862, at Pigeon Bay near the French Settlement at Akaroa, New Zealand. He was the youngest son of Captain and Mrs. Thomas Gay. He was educated at Punahou School, Hawaiʻi, England, Germany and the Mainland. He married Louisa Kala, granddaughter of High Chief Kainoahou, son of King Kaumualiʻi, the Last King of Kauaʻi.

They had eleven children: Amelia Dickson, Lawrence Kainoahou, Charles Ernest, Roland, Ralph, Elsie Greenland, May, Violet, Venus Holt, Louisa Blaisdell and Albert.

Charles Gay was the owner of the Island of Lanaʻi from 1902 to 1926. In 1926 he sold Lanaʻi to Dole Pineapple Company, the present owner. All of the Gay children were educated at Punahou School, Hawaiʻi. Lawrence, Charles, Roland, Ralph, May and Venus went on to Mainland colleges after Punahou School.

# CHARLES GAY

Charles Gay was born on January 8, 1862, at Pigeon Bay, near the French Settlement at Akaroa, New Zealand. He was the youngest son of Captain Thomas Gay and Jane Sinclair Gay.

# JANE SINCLAIR GAY

Jane Sinclair Gay, wife of Captain Thomas Gay and the eldest daughter of Elizabeth and Francis Sinclair was my grandmother. She was very kind, unselfish and helpful. She bought the island of Lana'i at auction in 1902 and presented it to her youngest son Charles, my father.

# CAPTAIN THOMAS GAY

Captain Thomas Gay was born in Crail, Fifeshire, Scotland. He married Jane Sinclair in 1848 and lived in New Zealand. He was a widower with two sons, James and Thomas by his previous marriage and five children with Jane Sinclair, his second marriage. Their children were George, Francis, Elizabeth, Charles and Alice, all of whom were born in New Zealand with the exception of Alice, their youngest, who was born on Ni'ihau.

Captain Gay owned a beautiful barque named 'Bessie' and took his bride on a honeymoon voyage to Australia and Van Dieman's Land. He built a beautiful home for his bride half a mile down the bay in New Zealand. After bringing the Sinclair and Gay families to Hawai'i, he returned to Australia to sell his barque, but became ill and died February 9, 1865 in New Castle.

The death of Captain Gay was reported in the New Castle Chronicle, February 11, 1865: "Captain Gay of the Barque 'Bessie' died, February 9, 1865 and was buried in the Presbyterian funeral grounds." The flags of all the ships in the harbor and about the town were displayed at half mast out of respect to the memory of Captain Gay. At four o'clock the funeral procession started from Mr. Mayo's, the body borne on a horse, and followed by nearly all the captains in port and other gentlemen walking by twos. The Reverend Mr. Coutts joined the procession and attended the body at the burial ground.

Registration of deaths has been compulsory in New South Wales since 1856, and records are held by the Registrar General's Department, Prince Albert Road, Sydney 2000. Captain Gay was a master mariner.

# ELIZABETH McHUTCHESON SINCLAIR

My great-grandmother Elizabeth McHutcheson Sinclair was born in Glasgow, Scotland, April 26, 1800. Her father was a prominent citizen of Glasgow and often entertained lavishly in their large beautiful home. She was her father's favorite child and often accompanied him on his business trips. She met my great-grandfather, Captain Francis Sinclair of the Royal Navy on one of these trips and they were married soon after.

# CAPTAIN FRANCIS SINCLAIR[1]

He was born in Edinburgh, the son of Sir George Sinclair and belonged to the Sinclair Clan of which the head of the family carried the title of the Earl of Caithness until 1920. A glance into medieval history of Scotland, it is interesting to know the story of the Sinclairs and St. Clair. When Ida E. Von Holt, a grand-daughter of Elizabeth Sinclair,

1. Excerpt from STORIES OF LONG AGO by Ida E. Von Holt

visited Scotland in 1936, she was fortunately rewarded in her search for the history of the Sinclair Clan. She obtained a small booklet about the family and the charter from which she quoted: "A certain Father Richard Hay, Prior of St. Pieremont, whose mother was married to Sir James St. Clair of Rosslyn, has left the only authentic information about the family of St. Clair. Being of an antiquarian turn of mind he made use of the opportunity afforded him of examining the various charters in possession of the family about the year 1700. These notes of the charters were published in 1835 under the title of the GENEALOGY OF THE SAINT-CLAIR OF ROSSLYN, including the Chartulary of Rosslyn. Unfortunately, a fire in the castle later destroyed all the old charters and papers.

The family descended from one Woldonius who took the name of Saint Clair from the place, probably in Normandy, where his estate was situated. He married a daughter of Richard, Duke of Normandy, father of William the Conqueror, and their son William accompanied his uncle The Conqueror to England and fought in the Battle of Hastings in 1066. Soon after that William Saint-Clair went to Scotland and served under the Scottish King Malcom Canmore. His grandson was "Dubbed" a Knight of King David I about 1138. The family was true to the Scotch Tradition and served under the Kings Malcom, David and Bruce."

The title, Earl of Caithness, from which our branch descended was first mentioned in 1358, and in 1481 the records show the first mention of the name as spelled Sinclair.

A Baron Sinclair was declared by Act of Parliament to be the chief of the St. Clairs. It seemed that the name of St. Clair was interchangeable in spelling with Sinclair.

In 1471, the estates of the powerful family were scattered among their sons who formed three branches of the family: The Lords St. Clair of Dysart, The St. Clairs of Rosslyn, and The Sinclairs of Caithness, whose title, Earl of Caithness, went to each succeeding eldest son.

In 1883, Francis Sinclair, my grand uncle who was then living at his home "The Pines" on Mt. Eden in Auckland, New Zealand, heard of the death, without heir, of the reigning Earl. Though he knew he was next of kin, he did not let himself be known, even though the English and Scotch papers advertised widely for an heir to come forward. He had previously been up in the north of Scotland, and had seen the estate near Aberdeen. The fine castle Dunbeath was going to ruin, and having no children, he did not wish to assume the responsibilities of the title, and to make his home in that part of Scotland.

A cousin of the late Earl, a barrister in London, was found and proved next of kin and took the title. He died in 1920 in Hollywood, California, without heirs, and was the last Earl of Caithness of our immediate Sinclair Clan.

To resume the story of Captain Sinclair of the Royal Navy; in 1815 after the battle of Waterloo, he had the honor of bringing the Duke of Wellington from Belgium over to England in his frigate of war, when off the cliffs of Dover a sudden squall hit the vessel. It was only Captain Sinclair's quick action at the tiller that saved the ship from going on the rocks. The great "Iron Duke" was on deck watching the whole scene, and after the ship had been safely brought into the harbor he expressed himself warmly, thanking Captain Sinclair for saving his life. Some weeks after, Captain Sinclair received a beautiful folding desk with a silver plate on it with the following inscription: "To Captain Francis Sinclair, in token of his splendid seamanship, and gratitude and esteem of the Duke of Wellington."

In 1819, on leave from his frigate of war, he was standing at the door of a small inn when a large coach and four drove up. On the high seat by the driver sat McHutcheson, my great, great-grandfather and beside him, his daughter Elizabeth. The moment Captain Sinclair set his eyes on her, he gallantly came forward to assist her down. She lingered over the descent, leaning on the handsome young captain. From then on the affair went to a speedy and happy ending.

Living at first in the outskirts of Edinburgh, Captain Sinclair felt uneasy at leaving his wife and small son George so far from neighbors, hence they moved to Stirling where they lived in a house called Bothwell Hall. It was situated near the wall of Stirling Castle and there five other children were born, making a group of six sturdy, happy children: George, Jane, Helen, James, Francis and Annie. Even though life seemed to have been happy and prosperous in Stirling, Captain and Mrs. Sinclair were seriously considering a tremendous change of scene.

Wonderful reports of the opportunities in New Zealand were being brought back to the old country. In October of 1839, with a number of other Scotch and English families, they decided to go to the new country. New Zealand was rapidly being opened up as an English colony and was finally declared such by the British Government in 1840. George, the eldest son, was then nineteen years old, Jane about sixteen and James fifteen years old. The second daughter Helen was thirteen, Francis was six years old and Annie seven months old.

Before leaving Scotland, Captain Sinclair had purchased land to be chosen in the North Island after his arrival in New Zealand. Unfortunately the government had not been able to secure the land from the Maoris, who were very fierce and wild in the North Island. Consequently, much time was taken up waiting for the arrangement.

They started out over land from Stirling to Glasgow and from there in a big sailing vessel to the new land beyond the horizon. The four month voyage 'round the Cape of Good Hope and past Australia and Van Diemen's Land, as Tasmania was then called, was an extremely hard and trying experience. They landed in Wellington in February of 1840.

The Sinclairs were charmed with Wellington, a simple, quiet community. Their settlement was near a Maori village. One day their two maids were busy washing and hanging their linens on the lines to dry (an accumulation from the long voyage) when a group of young Maoris came over and took away every bit of clothing, etc. Alfred Wallace, one of the young men who had accompanied the Sinclairs from Scotland prepared to run after them. He first went in to get his gun and Mrs. Sinclair stopped him at once saying, it would perhaps lead to an uprising on the part of the Maoris and urged him to wait until Captain Sinclair returned. That evening on being told the story, Captain Sinclair commended her foresight. The next day when he went down to the Maori village to see the chief (with whom he had already became acquainted), he was received with evident friendliness.

When the chief was told of what had happened he sent at once for the young marauders, ordering them to return every garment they had carried off the previous day. Then the old chief drawing his flax garments and blanket around him and with a pigeon feather stuck through the roll of hair on the top of his head, stepped out of his beautiful carved Wharre' (house) and signaled to Captain Sinclair. He would accompany him, and with great dignity he led the way and when everything had been returned, he took his huge spear, inlaid with abalone shell, and stuck it down in the ground at the front door. This, he said, shows my friendship to you. No one will molest you and your family while you are here. The spear remained in front of their door until they left Wellington in 1843.

After several exploring trips, Captain Sinclair decided to take his family and party in three large boats to see the land he thought of buying. They took tents with them and camped on shore every night. Captain Sinclair was alert to protect his family and party. A born leader, he seemed to have a sixth sense to warn him of any danger whether great or small. One night when all were asleep he heard, almost in his dreams, a strange cry which was unfamiliar. Rising at once to investigate, he realized the cry of a call, the Maori call of "Cooee." The hour was about four a.m., and on a distant hill outlined against the dawn-lit sky he saw a Maori woman waving her arms and giving that peculiar call which only a Maori could volume, and which could be heard for miles. The extraordinary behavior of the woman made the Captain suspicious. He awakened the family and the men sleeping under upturned boats. With rapidity and courage, they were packed and ready to move. The boats were launched and put out into the deep water.

Over the distant hill came literally a torrent of Maori men and women, all armed with spears and clubs, and though they made friendly gestures when they reached the shore and called "heremai," Captain Sinclair felt they were not to be trusted after such a warlike demonstration. So waving a farewell to them and signaling that they must go on, he commanded the men to put out to sea.

This and other experiences, as well as rumors of the unfriendly attitude of the tribe in that vicinity, made him decide against remaining and settling there. Returning to Wellington, he made an exchange and bought land in Pigeon Bay near Akaroa, Canterbury, on the South Island. For the voyage down the coast to the property, Captain Sinclair built a little sailing vessel and called it 'The Richmond.'

With Ebenezer Hay, a Scotchman and his family, the Sinclair Clan sailed down to Akaroa and on to Pigeon Bay in April 1843. This sturdy Scotchman and his wife were a great help in settling on the new property. For the first months the two families lived in tents and the schooner 'The Richmond' was sold for ten cows valued at twenty pounds per head. These cows were in Akaroa and to bring them over to Pigeon Bay, a trail had to be cut through the bushes. This was done on a line of the path used by the Maoris. It took eight men three weeks to make this trail wide enough to bring the cattle over as the old path used by the Maoris was difficult to find, except by an experienced bushman.

Captain Sinclair had won the confidence of the Maoris almost immediately and with their help was able to do much. While the road over the hills to Akaroa was being engineered, he had other men felling trees and sawing trunks into lumber. Captain Sinclair was a very resourceful man. He made nails out of copper and iron. His bellows was a cow's bladder, attached to a musket barrel. Nothing seemed impossible to Captain Sinclair and everyone who knew him would heartily agree.

By July 1843, a rough shack was built which the Sinclairs moved into. A year later, farther down the bay, a lovely house of white pine with red totara shingles was built, all cut from the forest by hand and under Captain Sinclair's supervision. It was named "Craigforth" after an estate in Scotland which they often visited. Except for the Hay family, there were no neighbors other than the Maoris.

At times a whaler would sail into port and Mrs. Sinclair and Mrs. Hay would make purchases for the needs of their families, but after the road over the hills was completed, no one thought it a hardship to walk the fifteen miles to Akaroa to see the shops. Mrs. Sinclair would often go as she was very fond of walking. In going over to Akaroa, she would be accompanied by her eldest son, George.

The years closely following their settling in Pigeon Bay were full and busy ones. Captain Sinclair planned well, buying sheep and cattle, planting and harvesting. Sailing ships brought seeds and grains, potatoes grew luxuriantly. The Maoris were friendly and helpful, and prosperous years followed to 1846 when Captain Sinclair decided to go to Wellington to make further purchase of land adjoining his estate.

One day he embarked for Wellington on a little schooner taking his eldest son, George and Alfred Wallace, who was engaged to his daughter Jane, my grandmother, then about eighteen years of age. Unfortunately the little schooner was lost at sea and nothing was heard from them nor was a trace of the schooner found. They were gone for months, so the family decided to sell their estate and move to other lands. Grandmother Sinclair was left a widow with five children. Her friends comforted her, and knowing what her husband had planned for the future of his family, gave her courage and faith in God to accomplish her husband's dreams. With friendly advice from Sir George Grey and her second son James, she managed her estate efficiently. Captain Sinclair's death was a great loss to his family and also to the colony of New Zealand. In 1862 the Craigforth home and estate were sold to Mr. Holmes.

In April 1863 the Sinclair and Gay families sailed from New Zealand in Captain Thomas Gay's barque 'Bessie.'

The vessel pictured above is similar in appearance to the barque 'Bessie' which was owned by Captain Thomas Gay.                    State of Hawaii Archives

# THE BARQUE 'BESSIE'

The beautiful barque 'Bessie' owned by Captain Thomas Gay, weighed 300 tons and was comfortably fitted for the long journey.

The barque was loaded with cattle, Arabian horses, Marino sheep, hay and grain for the animals, chickens, turkeys and peacocks. They also took provisions, jams, apples, books, clothing, furniture and a piano. They headed on a northerly course under the command of Captain Gay, who was knowledgeable with ocean traveling. He was able to change the course when it became too rough, and run with the wind to prevent the ship from rolling and pitching.

In order to relieve the monotony of such a long journey, Captain Gay would often sit with the family and tell them of the many sea tales and stories as told by his fellow mariners, many of which were fantasy

# PASSENGER LIST.

List of Passengers on board of Br. Barque
"Bessie" Thomas Gay Master; from
Port Angeles U.S.A bound to Honolulu

| NAME. | AGE. | COUNTRY. | OCCUPATION. |
|-------|------|----------|-------------|
| Mrs Gay | | | |
| Mrs Sinclair | | | |
| Mrs Robinson | | | |
| Mr Jas Sinclair | | | |
| Mr Francis Sinclair | 23 | | |
| Mrs F Sinclair | 22 | | |
| James Gray | 22 | | |
| Francis Gray | 9 | | |
| Geo Gray | 11 | | |
| Arthur Robinson | 9 | | |
| Eliza Gray | 6 | | |
| Charles Gray | 2 | | |

Th.ᵒ Gay, Master of

Bessie

Honolulu, Oahu, Sept 18 1863

rather than fact. One story in particular as told by some whaler friends of his, tells about the huge pieces of octopus as large as a man's thigh found in the bellies of sharks.

# TAHITI

Their first port of call was Tahiti. Their stay in Tahiti was a brief one, just long enough to replenish their supplies and pay their respects to the British Consul and the people of Tahiti. Continuing on their journey over the vast Pacific, the sight of the peaks of Mauna Loa and Mauna Kea on the island of Hawai'i was indeed a welcome sight.

After many arduous days at sea, they landed in Honolulu for a much needed rest and provisions, before continuing on to the Northwest.

# VICTORIA B.C.

The family arrived in Victoria in the early part of June, but settled there for only a short time as they were not impressed with this country for ranching, and also with the unfriendliness of the natives, so they moved on.

While in Victoria, they met Henry Rhodes, a kind gentleman who advised them to go back to Hawai'i and gave the Sinclairs and Gays a letter of introduction to his brother, Godfrey Rhodes who lived in Honolulu.

The ocean trip to Hawai'i was very rough but Captain Gay was very calm and manned the barque 'Bessie' efficiently and never left the tiller until they arrived in Honolulu, September 17, 1863. They were greeted by Reverend Samuel Damon who helped them with housing accommodations. Other members who were kind and helpful to them were Mr. Wyllie, Minister of Foreign Affairs, the Thomas Browns, Herman Von Holts, Bishop and Mrs. Staley, Mr. and Mrs. Synge and the Judds.

The list of passengers on board the barque 'Bessie,' arriving in Honolulu September 17, 1863, according to the Pacific Commercial Advertiser were: Elizabeth Sinclair, her sons James and Francis, and daughters Annie Sinclair, Helen Sinclair Robinson and son Aubrey, Jane Sinclair Gay, Captain Thomas Gay and their children: George, Elizabeth, Francis, Charles and Captain Gay's son by a former marriage.

Pictured to the left is the passenger list of the barque 'Bessie'. Captain Thomas Gay was master of the barque 'Bessie', Honolulu, Oahu, September 18, 1863.
Photo courtesy of the State of Hawaii Archives

A 7″ x 6″ pencil drawing by Fredda Burwell Holt of King Kamehameha IV, Queen Emma, and Prince Albert Edward Kauikeaouli.

Courtesy of Mr. and Mrs. John Dominis Holt

The family was very pleased with Hawai'i and the opportunity to meet the prominent large land owners from whom they negotiated land for ranching. They attended many functions sponsored by people of prominence including the Ali'i (nobility of Hawai'i).

They were invited to an elegant party given in honor of King Kamehameha IV and Queen Emma by Mr. and Mrs. Wyllie. It was at this party that the Sinclair family had an opportunity to ask the King for purchase of ranch land. The King offered land on O'ahu, stretching from the present site of the City Hall to Diamond Head for $10,000 in gold, but Mrs. Sinclair and her sons didn't care for this land because it was not suitable for ranching.

Most of Waikiki in those days was under water. They were also offered Kahuku on the island of O'ahu by Wyllie, Ford Island in Pearl Harbor, by Dr. Ford and all the adjoining lands of Honouliuli and Ewa, all of which could have been purchased reasonably. The family not finding what they wanted, decided to leave for California.

# THE PURCHASE OF NI'IHAU BY ELIZABETH SINCLAIR

When the King heard that the family was planning to go to California, he offered to sell the island of Ni'ihau to them if they would stay in Hawai'i. After investigating the island of Ni'ihau, they were so pleased with this little island that Mrs. Sinclair bought it for $10,000 in gold from King Kamehameha V, who had ascended to the Hawaiian throne in 1864.

Mrs. Sinclair, a woman of wealth, also purchased large tracts of land on the island of Kaua'i. She and her family lived on Ni'ihau for a few years before moving to Makaweli, Kaua'i.

She was very kind and helpful to the Hawaiians. She spent many hours nursing the sick and providing them with food and other necessities. The Hawaiians loved and respected her. She had always told her family that she wanted Ni'ihau to be kept in the true Hawaiian way of life. She wanted every one in the family to have a share of her estate.

# THE GEOGRAPHY OF NI'IHAU

Geologically, Ni'ihau was formed by the same volcano which created neighboring Kaua'i, making it one of the oldest of the Hawaiian Islands. It is a single lava dome, 1200 feet at its highest point and seventeen and a half miles southwest of the island of Kaua'i. It consists of 46,000 acres and is a semi-desert flat island, covered with brush, scrub and kiawe. There are sandy stretches, miniature lakes and thousands of wild turkeys are found in the upper regions.

The landings are Ki'i, Kaununu and Nonopapa. Ki'i landing, located on the eastern section of Ni'ihau, was used as the winter landing.

Island of Ni'ihau                    R. J. Baker, Bernice P. Bishop Museum

Nonopapa was the summer landing and was considered the best land-
ing on Ni'ihau. Kaumuhona and Keanahaki are the important bays.
It was in Keanahaki Bay that Captain Cook made his landing on
February 2, 1778.

Surf at Keanapuka, Ni'ihau.          State of Hawaii Archives

Dissected tuff cone (Kawaihoa), southern end of Ni'ihau.
W. D. Hohenthal, Bernice P. Bishop Museum

Nonopapa landing, island of Ni'ihau. Derrick will handle two ton. Summer landing only but best landing on the island.

W. D. Hohenthal, Bernice P. Bishop Museum Photo

Ki'i landing, Ni'ihau (Principle winter landing), small boats only can come along side pier.

W. D. Hohenthal, Bernice P. Bishop Museum Photo

Kaununui landing, Ni'ihau.    W. D. Hohenthal, Bernice P. Bishop Museum Photo

Sand hills south of 'Oiamoi, Ni'ihau.      W. D. Hohenthal, Bernice P. Bishop
                                                              Museum Photo

Kaiwaialoa                                    H. Von-Holt Photo

Keanauhi Valley, Ni'ihau.          W. D. Hohenthal, Bernice P. Bishop Museum

Looking north from Kaali cliff, island of Ni'ihau. Lehua island in the distance.
W. D. Hoenthal, Bernice P. Bishop Museum Photo

Poleho point, Ni'ihau looking north from (64.8-50.0). (Right)
W. D. Hohenthal, Bernice P. Bishop Museum Photo

Looking southeast from (62.5-57.00) elevation 200 feet. Keawe has cactus and meadow land.

W. D. Hohenthal, Bernice P. Bishop Museum Photo

Looking for shells.                    H. Von-Holt Photo

Ni'ihau Dam                                    H. Von-Holt Photograph

Kamilino, Ni'ihau (46.5-39.2).   W. D. Hohenthal, Bernice P. Bishop Museum Photo

Kaumuhona Bay, Ni'ihau. (Right)     W. D. Hohenthal, Bernice P. Bishop Museum

"City of Refuge" at Keawauoi Bay, Ni'ihau, (Left).

House of Refuge ca 1895, Ni'ihau.　　　

Above, Canoe House—Kamalino, Ni'ihau                    State of Hawaii Archives

Below, Remains of wreck of copra schooner Kona coast of Ni'ihau (53.9-38.2) schooner
was wrecked in 1918.           W. D. Hohenthal, Bernice P. Bishop Museum Photo

Cave dwelling Keanahaki Bay, island of Ni'ihau, front is thatched with grass. (See site 49, Kamalo, Lanai in "Island of Lanai" by Emory)

W. D. Hohenthal, Bernice P. Bishop Museum Photo

Houses at Kiekie, Ni'ihau ca 1910-1912.
J. F. G. Stokes, Bernice P. Bishop Museum Photo

Keanahaki bay, island of Ni'ihau. From (51.3-33.3) looking southeast. Point where Captain James Cook R.N. landed in person February 2, 1778. His boats first went ashore at Kahaino. Cottage is used by Mr. Robinson the owner, on fishing trips.

W. D. Hohenthal, Bernice P. Bishop Museum Photo

42

**GEORGE TAMOREE**

Drawing of Kaumaulii's son, George Tamoree. Hawaiian Mission Children's Society Photo

# FORMER OWNER OF NI'IHAU

Ni'ihau was owned by King Kaumualii up to the year 1810. King Kamehameha I made two attempts to conquer Kaua'i and Ni'ihau, but failed with heavy loss of lives, as evidenced by the dead that covered the beaches along the northeastern and eastern shores of Kaua'i. King Kaumualii ceded Kaua'i and Ni'ihau to King Kamehameha I to prevent further loss of lives.

According to information handed down by word of mouth, the island of Ni'ihau had a population in excess of five thousand inhabitants before the island was sold to Elizabeth McHutcheson Sinclair.

In those days, shortly after the early migration, the island was divided into several ahupuaas, each ruled by a high chief, usually a close relative of the King of Kaua'i. These chiefs made further divisions of land to chiefs of lower rank and the commoners.

All tenants were required to make their land productive in order to support the populace, because the rulers were very much against idle land.

The limited rainfall on Ni'ihau gave the Ni'ihauans incentive to search for ways and means of conserving moisture in the soil. Their problem was solved by the use of mulch. Pili grass, used for building and thatching huts, was also one of the means of conserving moisture, by adding humus to the soil during the process of decomposition.

The sweet potatoes and yams that were grown on Ni'ihau were very popular with the trading vessels and whaling ships of the late 18th century and early nineteenth century, because they lasted longer in storage than those purchased on Kaua'i and O'ahu.

# THE NI'IHAUANS

The men of Ni'ihau, tall in stature and powerful, were hired by the Robinsons to do various types of duties such as: collecting honey, tending the sheep and cattle, hitching wagons and loading supplies, driving turkeys, loading and handling whale boats and cleaning out some of the water holes. They were very religious and the tenet of the Sabbath being reserved for the Lord was reverently maintained and upheld.

The women, masters in the art of mat weaving and hat making, were unmatched by the other women of the Hawaiian Archipelago. The basic material used in this lost art was the Makaloa straw, an extract from the Makaloa plant, a specie of Cyperus found only on Ni'ihau and Kaua'i. It is a perennial sedge found in or near fresh or salt water. By a process, known only by the women of Ni'ihau and Kaua'i, they were able to utilize the upper and lower parts of the stems, to produce a product as flexible as cloth. It is from this product that floor and bed covers, clothing, capes, cloaks and even the finest loin cloths for Kings Kaumualii, Kamehameha I and Liloa were made.

The very rare and exquisite seashells of Ni'ihau (found nowhere else in Hawai'i or the South Seas) provide a very unique and fruitful supplement to their meager income. The women of Ni'ihau, noted for their patience and creativity, spend countless hours collecting, sorting, classifying and preparing these exotic seashells. The leis made from these shells are prized possessions throughout the world.

The present population of Ni'ihau is about 250, most of whom are pure Hawaiians. The language of the Ni'ihauans is Hawaiian, but their dialect is somewhat different from the Hawaiians on other islands. They pronounce "K's" as "T's." Words such as Kāua is Tāua, which means us, Kamali'i is Tamali'i, meaning children. This differential may be the result or reflection of the language of their forefathers or the homeland of the Hawaiians.

The people of Ni'ihau are very friendly, helpful, law abiding and resourceful. They are very conservative and protective of the elements that provide them with the necessities of life. If a fisherman went fishing, he would catch enough fish for his family for one day, and if he sees a wild pig in the course of his daily duties, he is allowed to stop and catch it. The pork is salted or dried and stored for future use.

Fish, lobsters and delicacies from the ocean are plentiful around Ni'ihau. The Robinsons provide the populace with fresh beef, turkeys and other provisions. Each family is given a house and sufficient land to cultivate into gardens or the raising of other produce.

# SPORTS OF THE NI'IHAUANS

The Hawaiians were a people of wisdom, energy and courage. They were very athletic and engaged in sports such as: wrestling, racing on foot and canoeing. Surfing was the sport of Hawaiian Kings. The men were excellent surfers. Some of whom were so skillful that they could touch a certain rock in the ocean as they went swiftly by.

They played games such as Ulumaika (bowling stones) and Konane (checkers). They knew how to travel by canoe from one island to another without the use of modern navigational instruments.

Fresh water pond, Ni'ihau.
All large ponds disappear
in summer.
W. D. Hohenthal, Bernice
P. Bishop Museum Photo

Shipping cattle,
Nonopapa landing.
State of Hawaii Archives

Wool shed from stone Quay Nonopapa, island of Ni'ihau. A small railway brings wool from shed.    Bernice P. Bishop Museum Photo

Fishing at Nahina— Hookanu, Ni'ihau.

State of Hawaii Archives

Loading sheep at Kii landing, Ni'ihau.

W. D. Hohenthal, Bernice P. Bishop Museum Photo

Loading sheep.                    Bernice P. Bishop Museum Photo

Village of Puuwai, island of Ni'ihau with Puu kaeo in background.
W. D. Hohenthal, Bernice P. Bishop Museum Photo

Typical house and water tank Puuwai Ni'ihau. Mr. Robinson, the owner builds a house of this type for each couple married on Ni'ihau. He retains the ownership of the house.

W. D. Hohenthal, Bernice P. Bishop Museum Photo

Manager's house, Ni'ihau.                    State of Hawaii Archives Photo

School children at Puuwai, Ni'ihau. Attendance January, 1924. Twenty girls, twelve boys up to fourth grade.

W. D. Hohenthal, Bernice P. Bishop Museum

# EDUCATION

There is only one school on the island of Ni'ihau, located in Puuwai and serving Grades 1 through 8. The school is under the State Department of Education. The officials of the Department of Education have a mutual understanding with the Robinson family regarding yearly visitation agreements. The officials are transported to Ni'ihau by the Robinson landing craft which is the only means of transportation to the little island. Upon landing on Ni'ihau, they are taken on a forty-five minute ride by truck to where the school is located.

The three teachers of the Ni'ihau School are natives of Ni'ihau, one of whom is Mrs. Keale who has a college degree and teaching certificate. The school consists of three one room buildings, and are equipped with standard text books and furniture. All instructions are in English, but Hawaiian is spoken at home, because it is the language of the island.

Upon graduating from the Ni'ihau School, students desiring to continue beyond the eighth grade, usually move in with relatives at Waimea, Kaua'i so they can attend high school or are given scholarships to attend Kamehameha Schools by the Robinson family.

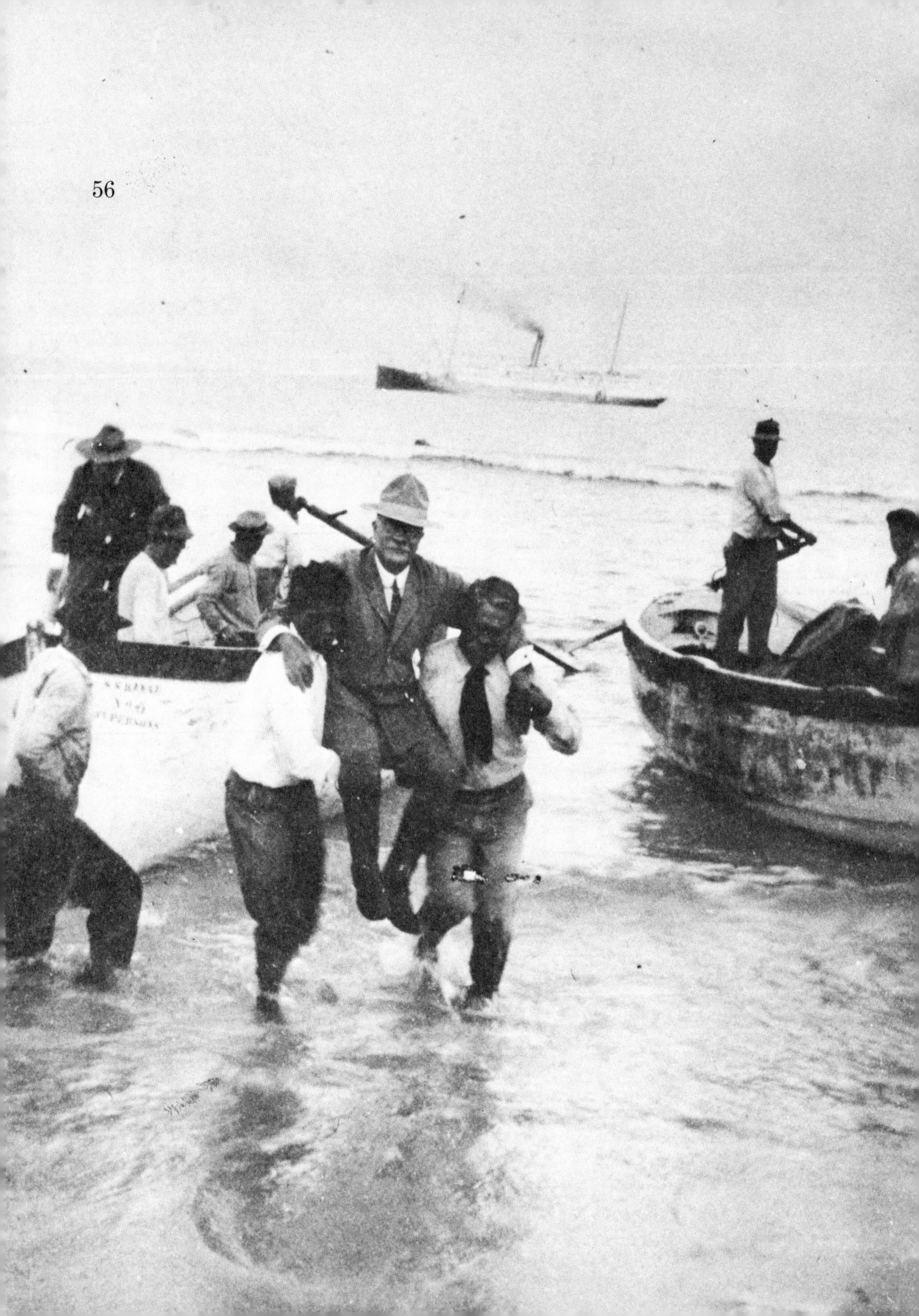

# TRANSPORTATION TO NI'IHAU

Visits to the remote, privately owned island of Ni'ihau are by invitation only. The Robinson family has provided hospitality to the school and health officials when business requires them to visit the island.

Newsmen and the curious are excluded from visiting Ni'ihau. The only means of transportation is by an old World War II landing craft owned by the Robinsons and can only accommodate eleven passengers.

The boat handles supplies for the people of Ni'ihau and also the island's produce. Whale boats are also used to carry passengers and produce to the inter-island boat anchored at the landing in Nonopapa once a week and also to the landing craft anchored a few feet from shore.

According to Hawaiian history, it indicates that Captain James Cook arrived at Ni'ihau on February 2, 1778 and anchored in Keanahaki Bay. His landing boats went ashore at Kahaino.

The Robinson beach cottage used on their fishing trips is located at Kahaino. There are sand hills south of Oimi, and a cave dwelling in Keanahaki Bay, the front of which is thatched with pili grass.

The village of Puuwai is the principle settlement of Ni'ihau, except for the Robinson homestead at Kiekie about two miles away.

The Robinson home in Kiekie was a typical old fashioned home. There were nineteen rooms, bathrooms, and many porches and passageways. The lumber of the main part of the house was brought by ship around Cape Horn from Boston in the year 1864. Servants' quarters, carriage shed, warehouses, and honey house were built nearby. There are miles of pasture land which were covered with grass and kiawe trees.

Mr. Von Holt and Ni'ihau men                                    H. Von Holt Photo

Hawaiians on
beach landing,
Nonopapa landing.

58

State of Hawaii
Archives Photo

BELOW: Steamer
arrivals and departures,
Nonopapa landing.

Bernice P. Bishop Museum Photo

S.S. Kinau at anchorage at Kii, Ni'ihau looking south from the landing.
W. D. Hohenthal, Bernice P. Bishop Museum Photo

# PEOPLE AND LEGENDS OF NI‘IHAU

60
My sister Amelia and I, still remember the names of some of the Ni‘ihauans who visited my mother whenever they came to Waimea. They were Niheu, Keale, Maui, Kanahele and Kaika. Whenever Kaika came to our home at Kikiaola, he usually rode on a beautiful white horse. His appearance was very dignified with his long white beard.

These people brought with them dried fish, black-eye susan leis and shell leis. In return, mother gave them poi, bags of flour, crackers etc. These are some of the stories as told by Kaika:

## KO-’ELI-LIMA-O-HALALI’I

According to Kaika, sugar cane grew from six to twelve feet under the sand. The Ni‘ihauans used to dig with their hands in order to get the cane. Ko—sugar cane; ’Eli—dig; Lima—hand; O—of: Halali’i—name of place.

## ’ULU-HUA-IKA-HAPAPA

(The Breadfruit Tree that grew flat and bore fruit on the ground)

He also spoke of the peculiarity in the growing habit of Ni‘ihau Breadfruit Trees. Instead of growing in an upright position, branches grew parallel with the ground with its fruit dangling on the ground. The Ni‘ihau women used to design patterns for their quilts after these freaks in the ’Ulu or the Breadfruit kingdom.

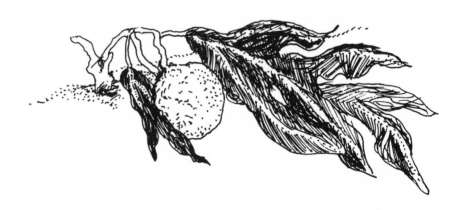

# THE DESTRUCTION OF THE AKUAS

The people of Kaua'i and Ni'ihau were accustomed to going to one end of Ni'ihau to fish. But it often happened that while they were sleeping on the sand after a hard day's fishing, the Akuas would come and devour many of the men.

One brave man decided that he would get rid of the Akuas. He built a long house similar to a canoe house, which had only one entrance. He made many Ki'is or wooden images of people. In the head of the images he placed mottled, gray and black eyes of 'opihi or mussel shells.

He put these images in the long house, concealing himself outside. At night the Akuas came out for their usual meal. Looking into the house, they saw the Ki'is with their shining eyes. At first they were surprised, but as the images lay very still, the Akuas decided that the Kaua'i men slept with their eyes open. They entered and tried to eat the images. Their teeth were caught in the wood and while trying to free themselves, the crafty Kaua'i man quickly closed the door and set the house on fire and all the cruel Akuas were burned to death. Thereafter, Ni'ihau became safe for fishermen and to this day this part of the island still bears the name of Ki'i.

# SHARKS OF NI'IHAU

During the time that Francis Sinclair was managing Ni'ihau, the sheep population was about 30,000. Mutton was not in demand, so after the shearing season, sheep were slaughtered and boiled down for tallow, because tallow was in great demand, in England as well as in the United States.

While the mutton was being boiled down, the offal was thrown into the ocean, which attracted sharks in great numbers. Uncle George Gay used to set out a shark hook and line to catch them. One of the Hawaiians came and told him that he would take the hook and line out to a mooring about one hundred feet from shore. He swam out, but before he reached the floater, he called out to pull the line, that a shark had taken the hook. When the shark was pulled ashore, it measured eight feet. This man took another line and tied it to the mooring and swam back to shore. Before reaching shore another shark was caught, which was also an eight footer. It would be hard to believe this story, but the Hawaiians on Ni'ihau believed wholeheartedly that the Ni'ihau sharks would never attack them. According to Uncle George, sharks were all around this man, but not one of them attacked him.

# KAPAHEE

In our conversation with Dad regarding seamanship among the Ni'ihauans, the name of Kapahee was always mentioned as outstanding in handling boats in the rough sea between Kaua'i and Ni'ihau. This man also had a general knowledge of the early navigational tactics and skills used on their ocean voyage to the South Seas. He knew what stars to follow on the way to Tahiti and return.

There was another interesting man, whose name I cannot recall. He had an unusual memory, although he could neither read nor write. When asked where did a certain man work on a certain day a year before, he could give you the answer in a few seconds. A check of the foreman's report would find he was right. On shipping days, when a man put a sheep on the boat he called out "Kahi", which meant One, the freight clerk would mark "1" on his pad, but this man kept it all in his head and when fifty was reached, he would stop the loading. Sometimes the freight clerk would claim that they had only forty-nine. A recount would be made and found that this man was correct. When you take into consideration that the early Hawaiians depended a lot on memory to pass on information from one generation to another by word of mouth, you could imagine how highly developed their memories must have been.

# PINEAPPLES ON NI'IHAU

My father, Charles Gay, told me that he had seen pineapples growing at the end of a stock twenty to twenty-five feet away from where it was originally planted. He brought some slips and planted them along the picket fence of our Kikiaola Home in Waimea, Kaua'i. These plants bore some very nice fruit about eighteen months after it was planted. They were much smaller than the pineapples we have now. The original Ni'ihau pineapples were brought in from the Marquesas Islands before 1850. The Pacific and Commercial Advertiser, July 2, 1856, mentioned that there were acres and acres of fruit.

# AUBREY ROBINSON

Aubrey Robinson, was the son of Helen Sinclair and Charles Barrington Robinson and one of the grandsons of Elizabeth Sinclair.

Mr. and Mrs. Aubrey Robinson, Ni'ihau.                    H. Von-Holt

He was born in Akaroa, New Zealand and received his law degree from Boston University.

He married Alice Gay, his first cousin who was the youngest daughter of Jane Sinclair and Captain Thomas Gay. They had five children: Sinclair, Selwynn, Aylmer, Eleanor and Lester.

Aubrey Robinson became owner of Ni'ihau and vast holdings on Kaua'i after Elizabeth Sinclair's death. After Aubrey's death, his son Aylmer took over the management of Ni'ihau and Kaua'i. The Lester Robinson family is the present owner of Ni'ihau.

# AYLMER ROBINSON

Alymer Robinson, eldest son of Aubrey Robinson and a graduate of Harvard University was appointed manager of the Ni'ihau Island after his father's death. He spoke fluent Hawaiian and was well liked and respected by the Ni'ihauans.

He helped to educate many of the children at Kamehameha Schools. Aylmer often told outsiders that visitors were not allowed to go to Ni'ihau because if visitors were allowed, many would exploit and spoil the islands' way of life. His one desire was that the Hawaiian way of life be perpetuated.

During Aylmer's management, he set up some rules for the Ni'ihauans such as: no smoking, no liquor and Sundays be dedicated to church activities only.

Hunting on the island is restricted to the inhabitants and outsiders had to acquire a permit from Aylmer to visit the island or the people.

After Aylmer's death, management of the estate and Ni'ihau was transferred to his brother Lester.

The present day managers and controllers of this vast estate are in the hands of Lester Robinson's sons, Keith and Bruce and his widow.

The visitation restrictions imposed by the Robinsons have caused many questions by outsiders. Many individuals and agencies have even resorted to devious and unscrupulous manipulations to eliminate these restrictions. The Robinson family has maintained a firm stand and have kept Ni'ihau and its people untarnished and in an environment that is the envy of a multitude of people.

There being no air fields on Ni'ihau, transportation to the island is restricted to water crafts and those receiving visitation permits and

The late Aubrey Robinson, former owner of Ni'ihau (left) and his son, the late Aylmer Robinson, for many years the manager of Ni'ihau Ranch (right).

W. D Hohenthal, Bernice P. Bishop Museum Photo

commuters, board the landing craft and after a four or five hour trip, disembark at the landing at Nonopapa.

Aylmer Robinson (in foreground) and party at Nonopapa.          H. Von Holt Photo

Buildings at Ki'i, island of Ni'ihau, looking north from the beach.
W. D. Hohenthal, Bernice P. Bishop Museum Photo

Front view of Robinson home at Kiekie, Ni'ihau.
W. D. Hohenthal, Bernice P. Bishop Museum Photo

Mr. Robinson's home at Kiekie, island of Ni'ihau.

W. D. Hohenthal, Bernice P. Bishop Museum Photo

# DECEMBER 7, 1941

The attack on Pearl Harbor on December 7, 1941 by Japan was not known by the Ni'ihauans because they did not have telephones, radios or any form of communication with Kaua'i. On this particular day a Japanese pilot crash landed on Ni'ihau and terrorized the Ni'ihauans. A very powerful man by the name of Kanahele, after being shot in the ribs, hips and groin by the pilot, picked him up and bashed him against a stone wall. Kanahele was taken to Waimea Hospital where he recovered and later returned to Ni'ihau.

On August 15, 1945, he was awarded the Medal of Merit and the Purple Heart Medal by Lieutenant General Robert C. Richardson, Jr., commander of the armed forces of the Middle Pacific. The details of this incident were published by the *Star-Bulletin*, December 16, 1941.